Submarines

Alex Frith

Designed by Zoe Wray

Illustrated by Emmanuel Cerisier and Giovanni Paulli
Edited by Jane Chisholm
Submarines expert: Commander Jonathan Powis RN

Contents

What is a submarine?

Submarines are ships that can travel underwater. They've been around for about a hundred years. The earliest ones could only dive for short bursts, but modern, nuclear-powered subs can stay underwater for months.

Basic parts of a nuclear submarine

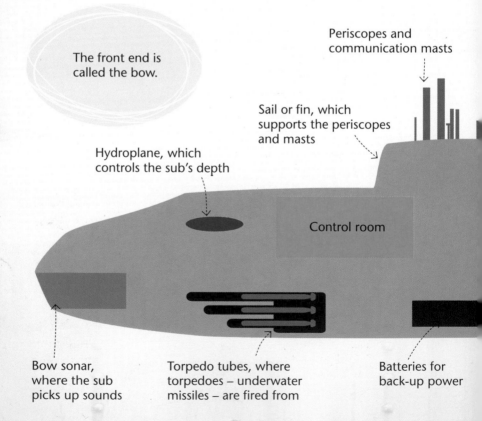

The front end is called the bow.

Periscopes and communication masts

Sail or fin, which supports the periscopes and masts

Hydroplane, which controls the sub's depth

Control room

Bow sonar, where the sub picks up sounds

Torpedo tubes, where torpedoes – underwater missiles – are fired from

Batteries for back-up power

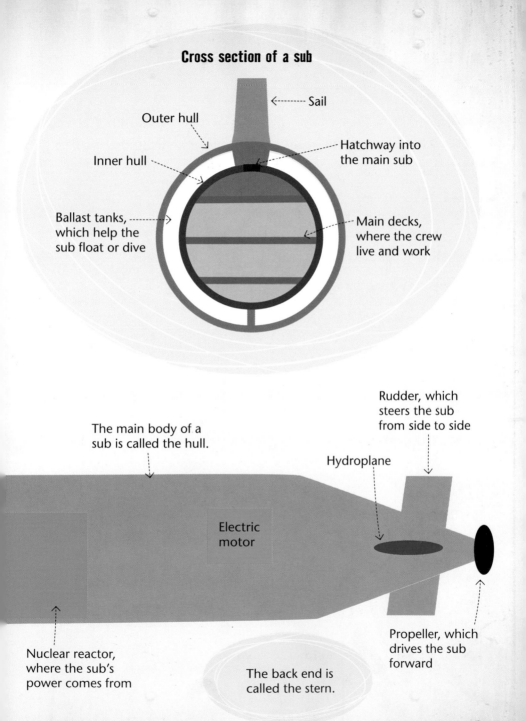

Cross section of a sub

Sail

Outer hull

Inner hull

Hatchway into the main sub

Ballast tanks, which help the sub float or dive

Main decks, where the crew live and work

Rudder, which steers the sub from side to side

The main body of a sub is called the hull.

Hydroplane

Electric motor

Nuclear reactor, where the sub's power comes from

The back end is called the stern.

Propeller, which drives the sub forward

Invisible enemies

The first submarines were designed to launch sneak attacks on enemy ships using underwater missiles. Modern subs can fire at targets on land, too.

Types of modern submarines

The biggest subs are SSBNs. SS means 'submarine'; B means they carry 'ballistic' nuclear missiles; N means they run on 'nuclear power'.

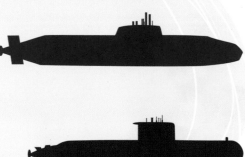

Smaller nuclear-powered SSNs don't carry ballistic missiles. They hunt enemy subs and carry troops to land in secret.

Not all subs are nuclear-powered. SSKs – the K stands for Killer – are diesel-powered. They wait silently for enemy subs and ships to come close.

Rugged explorers

Some subs are designed to explore. They look for shipwrecks, or study rocks and the eerie creatures that live really deep down.

Inside *HMS Astute*

Rudder

TOP SECRET! A silent propeller called a propulsor is attached to the stern. The way it looks and works is really secret, so it can't be shown here.

Storage space for machine spares and other supplies

Aft hydroplane – find out more on pages 12-13.

The propulsor shaft runs all through the aft of the sub.

Turbo generators for powering pumps and other machines

A nuclear-powered sub can run for over 20 years without needing to refuel.

Pipes to carry steam to and from the nuclear reactor

The hull is covered in rubber tiles that absorb sound. This makes it easier to hide from enemy ships.

TOP SECRET! The nuclear reactor that powers the ship is in here. The way it works is secret, but you can find out more on pages 16-17.

Turbines to drive the propulsor. Find out more on pages 16-17.

This is a watertight barrier, called a bulkhead. It can be sealed off in case of a flood.

A back-up diesel-powered generator for emergencies. Find out more on pages 16-17.

Engineers keep the engines turning and look after the reactor.

How deep can submarines go?

Most military subs can't go very deep, but some exploring subs can go to the very bottom of the ocean.

Submarine:	Max. depth:
Type U31 (Germany, 1914–1918)	
• One of the earliest working subs, used in the First World War	50m (164ft)
Astute class SSN (UK, 2007–present)	
• A modern nuclear-powered sub	at least 250m (800ft)
DSV _Shinkai_ (Japan, 1989–present)	
• A modern deep-sea exploring sub	6,500m (21,000ft)
Bathyscaphe _Trieste_ (Italy, 1953–1966)	
• An old deep-sea explorer designed to go as deep as possible	at least 11,000m (36,000ft)

The deepest ever dive was completed in 1960 by the _Trieste_. It went to the deepest part of the sea – the bottom of the Challenger Deep, part of the Mariana Trench in the Pacific Ocean.

Life on board *HMS Astute*

A tour of duty can last for three months. The crew splits into shifts, or watches, which take turns to operate the sub.

A view down the central corridor on the *Astute*

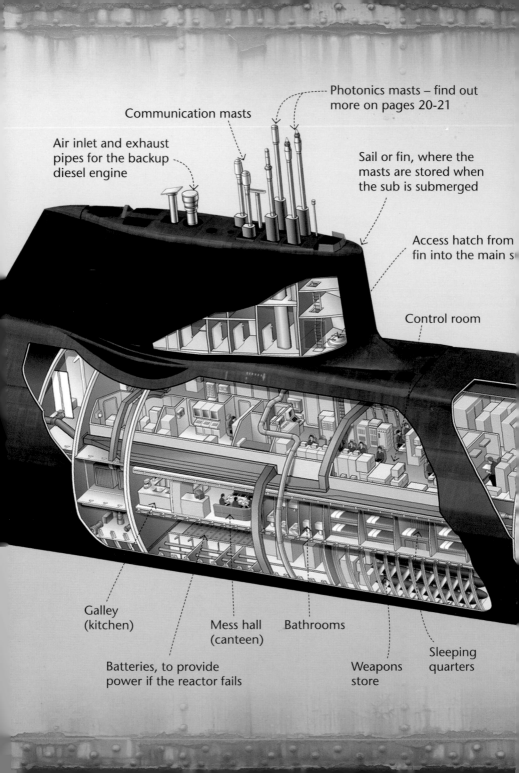

Communication masts

Photonics masts – find out more on pages 20-21

Air inlet and exhaust pipes for the backup diesel engine

Sail or fin, where the masts are stored when the sub is submerged

Access hatch from fin into the main s

Control room

Galley (kitchen)

Mess hall (canteen)

Bathrooms

Batteries, to provide power if the reactor fails

Weapons store

Sleeping quarters

Astute class (UK 2007-present)

- **Length:** 97m (318ft)
- **Speed:** 15kt surfaced; at least 25kt submerged
- **Crew:** 98

Speed in water is measured in nautical miles per hour, or knots (kt) for short. 1kt is about 1.85km/h or 1.15mph

the
b

Weapons hatch, where missiles and torpedoes are loaded

Forward hydroplane

TOP SECRET! A sonar array is hidden in the bow. The way it works is secret, but you can find out what it does on pages 22-23.

Office

Torpedo tubes. Find out how they work on pages 46-47.

High pressure air storage flasks

Here is *HMS Astute*, the first sub in the Astute class, being built at BAE Systems Marine Barrow Shipyard in Cumbria, England.

HMS Astute

One of the very newest types — or *classes* — of submarine is the Astute class, a British SSN. So far, just one has been launched: *HMS Astute*.

A typical day

06:00–08:30 The galley staff make breakfast for the watch coming on and the watch coming off.

06:30 The watch changes at 7. The oncoming watch have to get up, wash, dress and eat quickly.

07:00–13:00 The morning watch in the Control Room keep the sub moving and operating as quietly as possible.

13:00 Lunch and watch change. The outgoing watch can relax for a few hours.

14:30 A fire drill is run. Everyone must get to their stations quickly. It's one of many training exercises conducted regularly on board.

19:00 Another watch change. Some subs turn on red lights. It's still light enough to see, but this reminds the crew it's night-time.

Diving and surfacing

Subs can float on water because they carry lots of air.
To dive underwater, they need to let the air out.
Air is stored inside huge chambers called ballast tanks.

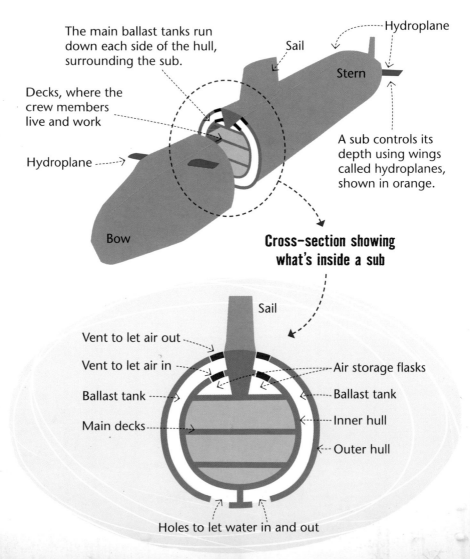

The main ballast tanks run down each side of the hull, surrounding the sub.

Sail

Hydroplane

Stern

Decks, where the crew members live and work

A sub controls its depth using wings called hydroplanes, shown in orange.

Hydroplane

Bow

Cross-section showing what's inside a sub

Sail

Vent to let air out

Vent to let air in

Air storage flasks

Ballast tank

Ballast tank

Main decks

Inner hull

Outer hull

Holes to let water in and out

Going down ... and coming back up

Vents open

⟵ Air

Water

1 The ballast tanks start out full of air so the submarine floats on the surface.

2 Vents open to let air out. This lets sea water flood into the tanks from below.

3 As the tanks fill with water, the sub starts to sink. When they're full, the sub will sit just below the surface.

4 To dive deeper, the hydroplanes are angled so water pressure pushes down on the front and up at the back.

5 To stay at the same depth, the hydroplanes must be level.

6 To come back up, they're angled the opposite way. Water pressure tilts the bow of the sub up.

7 To surface, the vents are closed, and air from storage flasks is forced back into the ballast tanks. This pushes water out of the bottom.

Water

8 As the tanks fill with air, the submarine rises.

Air storage flasks

Vents closed

HMS Astute just after it has dived

Once a sub has dived deep, there's no way to get air from the surface. Instead, air is made on board.

How does the crew breathe in a submarine?

A process called electrolysis is used to extract oxygen from sea water, so the crew always has air to breathe. Chemicals called scrubbers absorb the carbon dioxide they breathe out.

Diagram of a swim-out chamber

Outer hatch to the sea

Water floods in here.

Water flows out from here into the sub's drains.

Inner hatch

How to get out of a submerged sub

To get out (and back in), submariners go through a *swim-out chamber*. The chamber has to be flooded with water – so the pressure inside matches the pressure outside – before the hatch can be opened.

Swim-out chamber on the *Astute*

Outer hatch of the swim-out chamber on the *USS Hawaii*, a Virginia class SSN

Swim-out chamber on the *Hawaii*

This submariner is about to practice making repairs to the outside of a submerged sub.

Engine room

The engine provides power for the propeller, charges up the batteries, and makes sure there is fresh air, lighting and heating for the crew.

Engine parts of an SSN

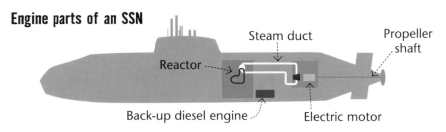

Reactor · · · · · >

Steam duct

Propeller shaft

Back-up diesel engine

Electric motor

Nuclear power

Nuclear subs get their power from a reactor, which contains uranium. Uranium is radioactive, which means it slowly breaks apart, and gets very hot, providing power. Here's how it works:

1 The hot reactor heats water in a short pipe.

2 This hot water pipe passes through a boiler. Water in the boiler turns to steam.

3 The steam passes through a turbine, which drives the motor.

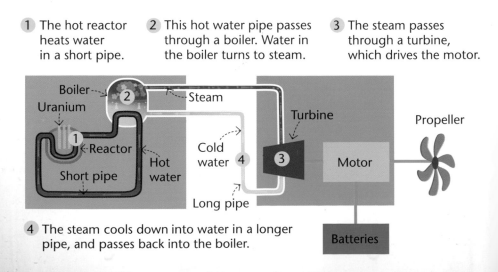

Boiler · · ·
Uranium

2

Steam

Turbine

Propeller

1

Reactor

Hot water

Cold water 4

3

Motor

Short pipe

Long pipe

Batteries

4 The steam cools down into water in a longer pipe, and passes back into the boiler.

Valve to
release
pressure

Cylinders where
fuel is burned

This shows part of the
engine inside the *USS Becuna*,
a diesel-electric sub used
during the Second World War.

Diesel-electric power

Most non-nuclear subs get power by burning diesel fuel
to power an electricity generator. This charges up the
batteries. Diesel-powered subs run their engines when
they're on or near the surface and can vent exhaust
fumes. When they're submerged, they run on batteries.

Seeing out

Many subs have a periscope – a long tube stored inside the sail. The crew can raise it above the waves to look for ships without having to surface.

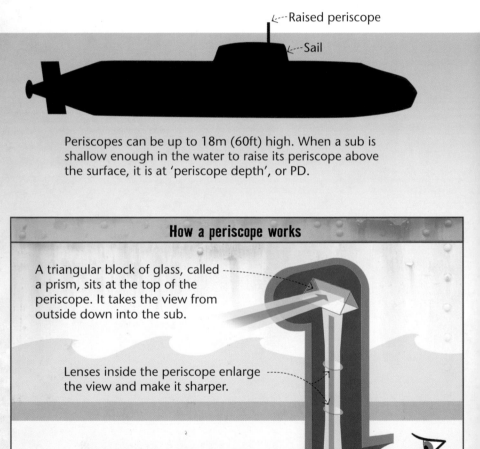

←---Raised periscope

←---Sail

Periscopes can be up to 18m (60ft) high. When a sub is shallow enough in the water to raise its periscope above the surface, it is at 'periscope depth', or PD.

How a periscope works

A triangular block of glass, called a prism, sits at the top of the periscope. It takes the view from outside down into the sub.

Lenses inside the periscope enlarge the view and make it sharper.

Another prism takes the view around the corner, so it can be seen through an eyepiece.

Eyepiece

What the captain sees

1 It's the captain's job to identify any ship spotted through the periscope.

2 If he can identify the ship, he'll know how tall the mast is, and how long the ship is.

3 He can compare the mast to marks on the eyepiece, to determine how far away the ship is.

4 These lines help him calculate how fast the ship is moving.

This view through the periscope of a Second World War sub shows a Japanese destroyer sinking slowly after a torpedo hit.

This periscope belongs to a German sub spotted on patrol in the North Atlantic during the First World War.

Submarine masts

The very latest submarines don't have periscopes. Instead, they use electronic devices called photonics masts. These work like digital video cameras.

Masts are operated from the sub's Control Room.

Control Room

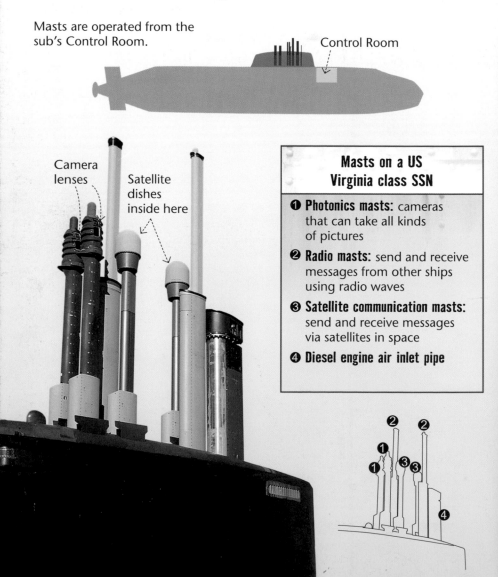

Camera lenses

Satellite dishes inside here

Masts on a US Virginia class SSN

❶ **Photonics masts:** cameras that can take all kinds of pictures

❷ **Radio masts:** send and receive messages from other ships using radio waves

❸ **Satellite communication masts:** send and receive messages via satellites in space

❹ **Diesel engine air inlet pipe**

Night vision

Photonics masts use cameras to take different kinds of images, especially to help see in the dark. Each image can be seen on a screen in the sub's Control Room.

This screen shows the view through a camera that picks up low-level lighting.

Even at night, enough light is detected to produce this green image. It shows the sub's own stern.

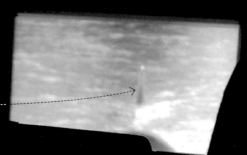

This screen is divided into sections.

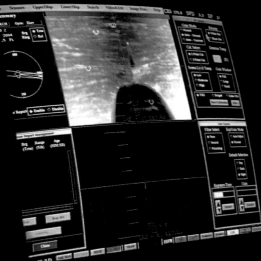

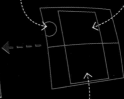

This section shows the stern of the sub as seen through a night-vision camera that detects infra-red light.

This section shows the position of the sub below sea level.

This section shows the view through a normal camera – nothing but darkness.

Seeing with sound

Most subs don't have windows. Deep underwater, crew members listen out, using a technique known as passive sonar.

How passive sonar works

Subs use underwater microphones called hydrophones to pick up sounds.

Passive sonar makes no noise, so it doesn't give away a sub's position.

Hydrophones in the bow of the sub pick up noises in front.

Most modern subs tow a long series of hydrophones behind them. This is called a 'towed array'.

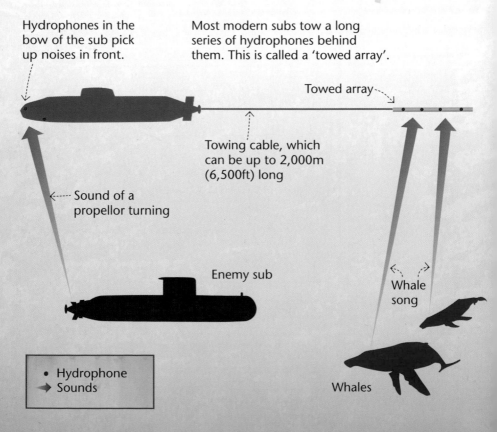

Towed array

Towing cable, which can be up to 2,000m (6,500ft) long

Sound of a propellor turning

Enemy sub

Whale song

• Hydrophone
➔ Sounds

Whales

In the sound room

The crew members who listen to the sounds picked up by hydrophones are called sonar operators.

What the sonar operator sees:	What the sonar operator hears:
Sounds converted into lines on a computer screen	A series of noises, from another sub, or from something else
• Each line represents a continuous sound coming from one source. • If the sound continues, the line keeps moving. • If the sound is getting louder, the line will get thicker.	• If it's a ship or sub, the operator should make out the propeller. • The beat of the propeller tells him how fast the ship is moving. • If the beat gets louder, it means the ship is getting closer.

Sending signals

Subs on or near the surface can send and receive messages using radio waves. But these can't travel far underwater, so submerged subs use other methods.

How to alert a submerged sub

A ship can try to contact a sub by dropping an electronic device called a bellringer into the sea.

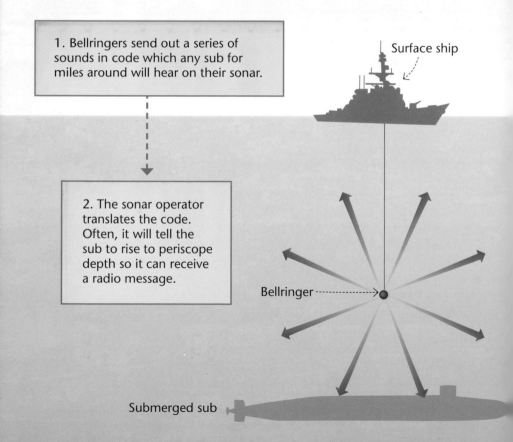

1. Bellringers send out a series of sounds in code which any sub for miles around will hear on their sonar.

2. The sonar operator translates the code. Often, it will tell the sub to rise to periscope depth so it can receive a radio message.

Surface ship

Bellringer

Submerged sub

Submarines at war

Here are a few examples of famous military submarine classes. Until 1954, all military subs were diesel-powered.

Early 20th century 1901–1913

The first ever submarine fleet was commissioned by the British Royal Navy in 1901. The subs were based on a prototype built by American inventor John Holland.

Five Holland Class subs were sent to attack the Russian Navy in 1905, but were recalled before any combat took place.

Holland Class (UK, 1903–1914)

- **Length:** 19.5m (64ft)
- **Speed:** 8kt surfaced; 7kt submerged
- **Crew:** 8

Type VIIC (Germany, 1941–1945)

- **Length:** 67m (220ft)
- **Speed:** 17.6kt surfaced; 7.7kt submerged
- **Crew:** 52

Over 550 Type VIIC subs were built between 1940 and 1944, more than any other used in the War.

The unique *Surcouf* was one of the biggest subs in the Second World War. It sometimes carried prisoners captured from enemy ships.

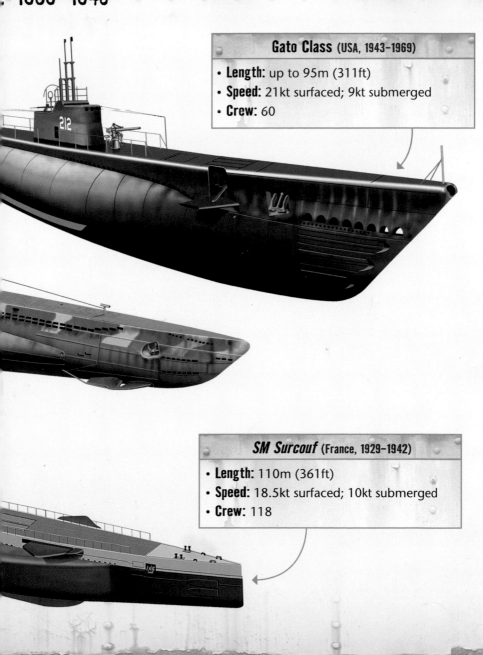

Gato Class (USA, 1943–1969)

- **Length:** up to 95m (311ft)
- **Speed:** 21kt surfaced; 9kt submerged
- **Crew:** 60

SM Surcouf (France, 1929–1942)

- **Length:** 110m (361ft)
- **Speed:** 18.5kt surfaced; 10kt submerged
- **Crew:** 118

How can a sub contact people on the surface?

A sub in distress sends up a large, bright buoy that broadcasts a loud signal for help.

A sub that wants to send a secret message can use a tiny, almost invisible buoy.

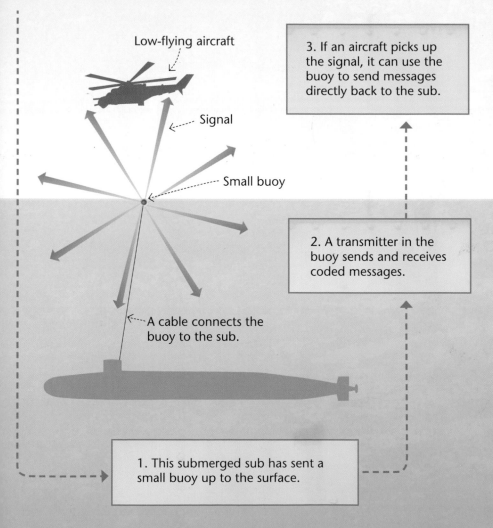

Low-flying aircraft

3. If an aircraft picks up the signal, it can use the buoy to send messages directly back to the sub.

Signal

Small buoy

2. A transmitter in the buoy sends and receives coded messages.

A cable connects the buoy to the sub.

1. This submerged sub has sent a small buoy up to the surface.

The First World War

When the First World War broke out in 1914, some navies had already developed small fleets of attack submarines.

U-boats

At first, Germany used its subs, known as U-boats, to attack supply ships. But in May 1915 a U-boat torpedoed the passenger liner *Lusitania*. This helped persuade the USA to join the war on Britain's side.

American newspapers were appalled that a number of American citizens, including some children, had died on board the *Lusitania*.

USS *Nautilus* SSN-571 (USA, 1954-1980)

- **Length:** 97.5m (320ft)
- **Speed:** 22kt surfaced; 25kt submerged
- **Crew:** 105

The *Nautilus* was the world's first nuclear-powered sub. It was named after the sub from Jules Verne's story *20,000 Leagues Under The Sea*.

21st ce

Type 214 SSK (Germany, 2004-present)

- **Length:** 65m (210ft)
- **Speed:** 12kt surfaced; 20kt submerged
- **Crew:** 27

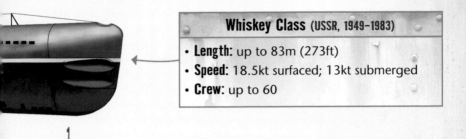

Whiskey Class (USSR, 1949–1983)

- **Length:** up to 83m (273ft)
- **Speed:** 18.5kt surfaced; 13kt submerged
- **Crew:** up to 60

During the Cold War, the rival navies of the USA and the USSR built up huge fleets of nuclear submarines. But they never saw actual combat.

571

ntury

Type 214 subs are diesel-powered, but they can stay submerged for weeks at a time, using an AIP (air-independent-propulsion) drive.

27a

First World War 1914–1918

The E class was the main class of
submarine used by the Royal Navy
during the First World War.

E Class (UK, 1912–1921)

- **Length:** up to 55m (181ft)
- **Speed:** 15kt surfaced; 10kt submerged
- **Crew:** 30

One Type U31 sub,
known by its serial
number *U-35*, was the
most successful sub in
the First World War.
It sank 224 ships.

Type U31 (Germany, 1914–1917)

- **Length:** 64.7m (199ft)
- **Speed:** 16.4kt surfaced; 9.7kt submerged
- **Crew:** 35

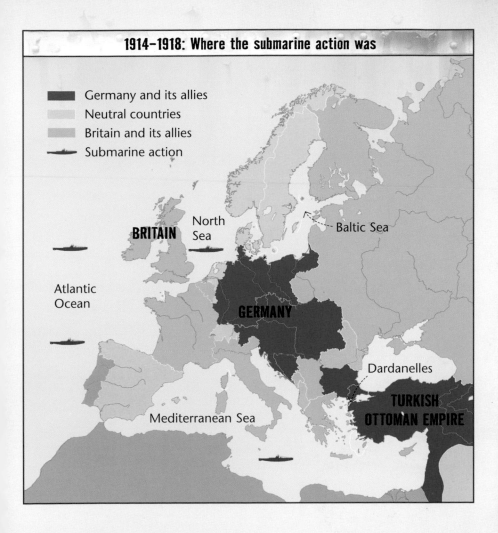

1914–1918: Where the submarine action was

Germany and its allies
Neutral countries
Britain and its allies
Submarine action

BRITAIN

North Sea

Baltic Sea

Atlantic Ocean

GERMANY

Dardanelles

Mediterranean Sea

TURKISH OTTOMAN EMPIRE

Anti-submarine warfare

Navies on both sides defended their ports from subs using nets and mines – explosives set to go off when hit.

Warships attacked subs using a new type of underwater bomb, called a depth charge. This exploded underwater, damaging a sub even if it didn't hit the hull directly.

Hero of the Dardanelles

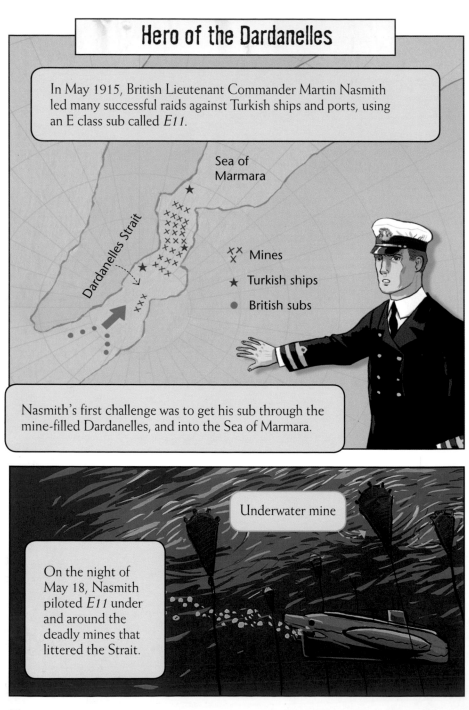

In May 1915, British Lieutenant Commander Martin Nasmith led many successful raids against Turkish ships and ports, using an E class sub called *E11*.

Sea of Marmara

Dardanelles Strait

×× Mines

★ Turkish ships

● British subs

Nasmith's first challenge was to get his sub through the mine-filled Dardanelles, and into the Sea of Marmara.

Underwater mine

On the night of May 18, Nasmith piloted *E11* under and around the deadly mines that littered the Strait.

Once in the Sea of Marmara, Nasmith captured a Turkish ship and strapped it to the side of *E11.* This disguise helped the sub to stay hidden from enemies watching from Turkish ports.

On a second raid, Nasmith stalked and destroyed an enemy warship, *Bosphorus.*

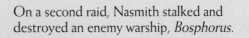

BOOM!

In three months, Nasmith and *E11* damaged a major port, and destroyed 85 ships. Nasmith was awarded the Victoria Cross medal for bravery.

The Second World War

Soon after the Second World War broke out in 1939, the Germans sent a fleet of U-boats into the Atlantic. They attacked enemy ships in deadly groups that the British called wolf packs.

Hunting U-boats

At first, most U-boats escaped undetected. But in time a team of British and Polish codebreakers cracked the Enigma code – a system the Germans used to send secret messages to their base. Codebreakers soon helped the Royal Navy locate hidden U-boats.

1942–1945: Where the main submarine action was

USSR
(RUSSIA)

UK

GERMANY

JAPAN

USA

Atlantic
Ocean

Pacific
Ocean

Germany, Japan and
occupied territory

Neutral countries

Britain, USA and allies

Sub action

An American warship in the Atlantic
Ocean drops a depth charge to
destroy a German U-boat.

Living in a U-boat

Submarine and U-boat crews could be out to sea for as long as 50 days. Each man only had one set of clothes for the entire voyage. Water was strictly rationed, so they hardly ever bathed. It was very smelly.

Space was so restricted that most men had to take it in turns to sleep in a bunk. Many even had to eat and sleep beside the torpedo tubes.

War in the Pacific

The USA joined the war in December 1941, after the Japanese attacked an American base at Pearl Harbor in Hawaii. They used mini subs and bombers launched from aircraft carriers.

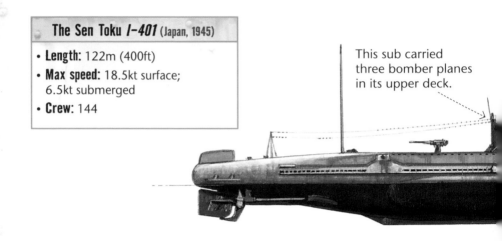

The Sen Toku *I–401* (Japan, 1945)

- **Length:** 122m (400ft)
- **Max speed:** 18.5kt surface; 6.5kt submerged
- **Crew:** 144

This sub carried three bomber planes in its upper deck.

The Japanese Sen Toku class was the biggest of the war, although it never saw combat.

America strikes back

The USA sent a fleet of large, fast, modern subs into the Pacific. Fitted with the latest sonar and radar they found and destroyed more Japanese ships than any other part of the US Navy.

The most successful sub in the war was the *USS Barb*. It destroyed over 50 ships, and even one train.

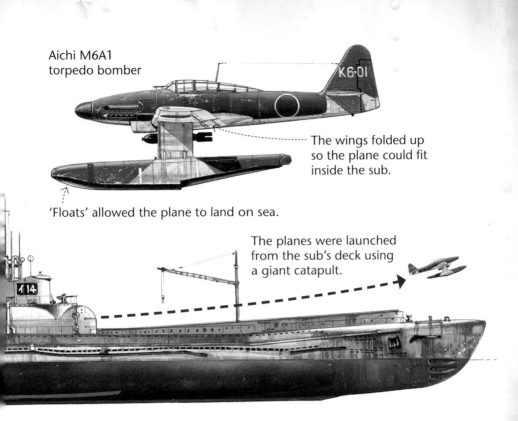

Aichi M6A1
torpedo bomber

K6-01

The wings folded up
so the plane could fit
inside the sub.

'Floats' allowed the plane to land on sea.

The planes were launched
from the sub's deck using
a giant catapult.

Final tally

Submariners in the Second World War destroyed huge
numbers of ships, but they paid a heavy price. More than
half of them – about 35,000 men – died at sea.

Final tally of submarine damage at the end of the war		
Country	Enemy ships sunk	Submarines lost
Germany	2,850	758 (80% of the fleet)
USA	1,079	52 (18% of the fleet)
UK	493	73 (32% of the fleet)
Japan	184	128 (75% of the fleet)

Miniature submarines

During both world wars, many countries built miniature submarines, known as midget subs, which could sneak more easily past mines and into ports.

One of the most successful was a British midget sub known as the *X-Craft*.

Propeller

Engine

The *X-Craft* (UK, 1942–1945)

- **Length:** 15.62m (51.25ft)
- **Max submerged speed:** 5.5kt
- **Crew:** 4

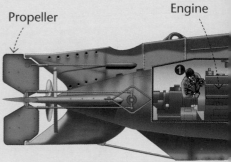

Torpedo subs

Some torpedoes were converted into short-range underwater vehicles. Men in diving suits sat on top.

The *Maiale* (Italy, 1918–1945)

- **Length:** 7.3m (24ft)
- **Max. submerged speed:** 4.5kt
- **Crew:** 2

Breathing masks

Detachable explosive

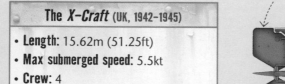

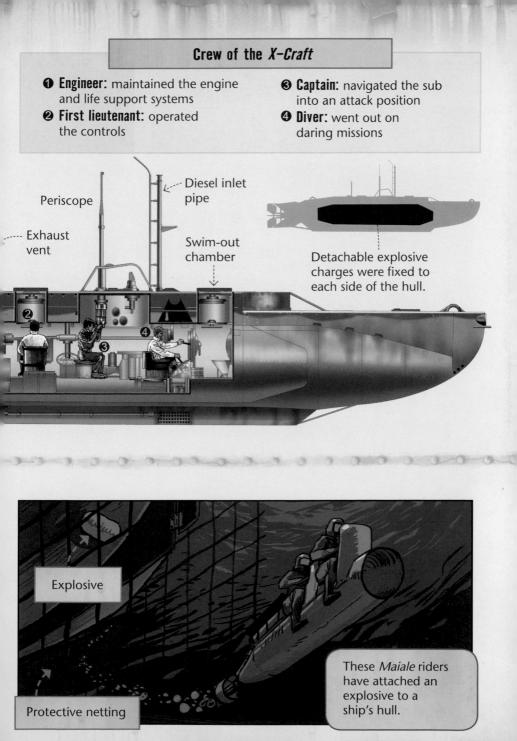

Crew of the *X-Craft*

❶ **Engineer:** maintained the engine and life support systems

❷ **First lieutenant:** operated the controls

❸ **Captain:** navigated the sub into an attack position

❹ **Diver:** went out on daring missions

Periscope

Diesel inlet pipe

Exhaust vent

Swim-out chamber

Detachable explosive charges were fixed to each side of the hull.

Explosive

Protective netting

These *Maiale* riders have attached an explosive to a ship's hull.

The *X–Craft* in action

X-Craft was towed behind a full-sized submarine called a mother sub. This journey, to a target in the Atlantic, the Mediterranean or Pacific, might take weeks.

Mother sub

During the journey, a 'passage crew' sat inside the *X-Craft*. Once they reached the target, they switched with an 'operational crew' who were on board the mother sub.

The operational crew detached the *X-Craft* from the mother sub, and went on alone, often towards a crowded enemy port.

One man on board was the diver.

He got out through the swim-out chamber and went off on daring solo missions.

Sometimes he had to cut through metal nets that protected ships in ports.

Another mission might be to destroy enemy telephone cables.

X-Craft also blew things up. It dropped its explosives under enemy ships...

...and sped away as quickly as possible.

Going nuclear

In 1954, the USA launched *USS Nautilus*, the world's first nuclear-powered sub. Soon, the USSR began to build its own. The two rivals competed to build the biggest, fastest and stealthiest subs.

Ohio class SSGN (USA, 1980–present)

- **Length:** 170m (560ft)
- **Max. speed:** 12kt surfaced; 25kt submerged
- **Crew:** 155

Nuclear-powered SSBNs carry nuclear weapons. Since 2002, some SSBNs have been adapted so they carry different, non-nuclear missiles. These are known as SSGNs.

This Ohio class sub was once an SSBN, but has been converted to an SSGN.

This is an artist's impression of missiles being launched from an Ohio class sub.

The world's largest submarine is a Russian SSBN in the Akula class (also known as Typhoon class). It's as big as a battleship.

Missiles are launched through hatches along the top of the sub.

This is an Advanced SEAL Delivery System. It's a detachable mini-sub used to carry special forces to battle zones in secret.

Around the world

Nuclear submarines can travel for months without needing to surface, making it easier to hide from ships and satellite cameras.

In 1960, *USS Triton* was the first sub to sail around the world fully submerged. It took 61 days.

Nuclear sub *USS Honolulu* has encountered a pair of polar bears after breaking through surface ice near the North Pole.

Secret technology

So far, only six countries have the know-how to develop nuclear submarines.

Nuclear submarine classes		
Country	SSBN	SSN
China	• Xia • Jin • Tang (under construction)	• Han • Shang
France	• Le Triomphant	• Rubis • Barracuda
India	• Arihant	None yet
Russia	• Akula / Typhoon • Delta • Borei	• Sierra • Shchuka / Akula • Yasen / Graney
UK	• Vanguard	• Trafalgar • Astute
USA	• Ohio	• Los Angeles • Seawolf • Virginia

Torpedoes

Most subs attack enemy ships using torpedoes – explosives that speed under the waves, set to detonate when close to their target.

Torpedoes are fired from torpedo tubes.

Most SSNs have tubes on either side of the bow.

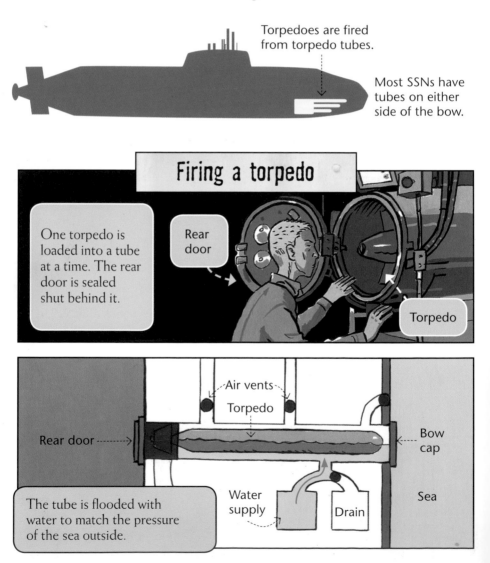

Firing a torpedo

One torpedo is loaded into a tube at a time. The rear door is sealed shut behind it.

Rear door

Torpedo

Air vents

Torpedo

Rear door

Bow cap

The tube is flooded with water to match the pressure of the sea outside.

Water supply

Drain

Sea

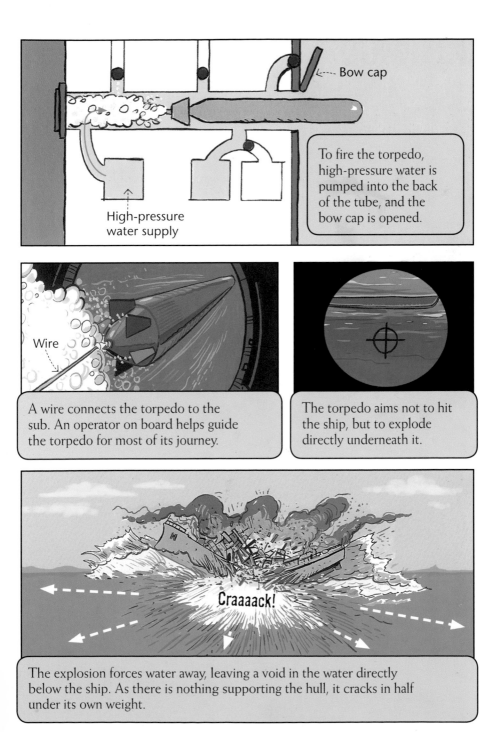

Bow cap

To fire the torpedo, high-pressure water is pumped into the back of the tube, and the bow cap is opened.

High-pressure water supply

Wire

A wire connects the torpedo to the sub. An operator on board helps guide the torpedo for most of its journey.

The torpedo aims not to hit the ship, but to explode directly underneath it.

Craaaack!

The explosion forces water away, leaving a void in the water directly below the ship. As there is nothing supporting the hull, it cracks in half under its own weight.

Missiles

Some subs carry flying weapons called missiles. These can hit targets on land, thousands of miles away.

The Ohio class SSBN has 2 rows of 12 missile hatches. Each missile is as tall as the hull.

Missiles are operated from the missile control compartment.

Small missiles can also be launched through torpedo tubes.

Cruise missiles

Cruise missiles have a powerful explosive in the tip. They're driven by a computer instead of a pilot, and fly very low to the ground to avoid detection.

A Tomahawk cruise missile

Tomahawk cruise missile (USA, 1983–present)

- **Top speed:** 880km/h (550mph)
- **Length:** 5.5m (18ft)
- **Weight:** 1,440kg (3,200lbs)
- **Range:** 1,600km (1,000 miles)

Nuclear missiles

SSBNs carry missiles with nuclear explosives, called ballistic missiles. They're fired up into the air like rockets.

A Trident II ballistic missile

The nuclear explosive is in here.

Ballistic missiles travel all the way up into space, before falling back down to Earth to hit their target.

Trident II ballistic missile (USA, 1990-present)

- **Top speed:** 29,000km/h (18,000mph)
- **Length:** 13.4m (44ft)
- **Weight:** 58,500kg (129,000lbs)
- **Range:** 11,300km (7,000 miles)

Oceanography

Oceanography, also known as marine science, is the study of the seas and oceans, and the things that live there.

Oceanographers explore the deep using submersibles – subs that need support from a mother ship on the surface.

Deep Rover (USA, 1994–present)

- **Length:** 3.3m (11ft)
- **Capacity:** 2 people
- **Max. depth:** 4,000m (13,120ft)

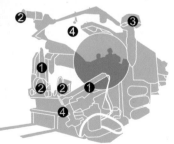

❶ Robotic arms for collecting samples from the seabed

❷ Bright lights to enable clear views

❸ Sonar sensors to make images of the seabed below

❹ Cameras to record the voyage

The submersible *Deep Rover* begins a dive in the Atlantic Ocean.

Robot submarines

Some subs, known as ROVs (or Remotely Operated Vehicles), are unmanned. They're controlled by an operator on board a mother ship or sub.

ROV *Super Achille* is collecting objects found in an ancient shipwreck at the bottom of the Mediterannean Sea.

ROV *Super Achille* (France, present day)

- **Length:** 72cm (2ft 5in)
- **Max. depth:** 1,000m (3,279ft)
- **Attachments:** cameras, lights, sonar

The ROV is connected to its mother ship by a tether.

COMEX-PRO

Undersea explorers

Here are some of the different types of submersibles, submarines and other vehicles used to explore the hidden world under the sea.

Farralon Diver Propulsion Vehicle
(Canada/USA 2004–present)

- **Max. depth:** 100m (330ft)
- **Capacity:** 2 divers
- **Submerged speed:** 2.8kt
- **Use:** for divers who need to travel long distances underwater

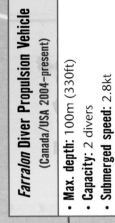

LS 370 Wet Bell
(South Africa 2002–present)

- **Max. depth:** 100m (330ft)
- **Capacity:** 2 divers
- **Use:** for lowering divers to the sea bed, often for salvage work

The *URF* is the world's largest rescue submarine.

URF rescue submersible
(Sweden 1979–present)

- **Max. depth:** 460m (1,510ft)
- **Capacity:** 4 crew; 35 rescuees
- **Submerged speed:** 3kt
- **Use:** for rescuing trapped submariners

Bathysphere
(USA 1928–1936)

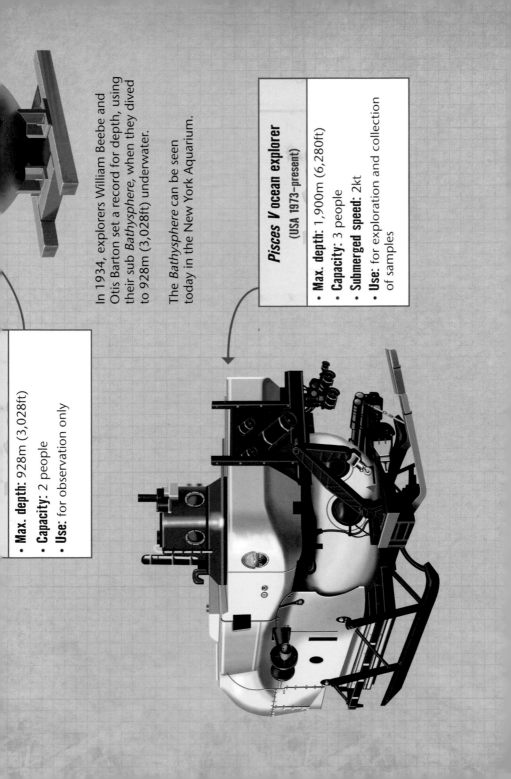

- **Max. depth:** 928m (3,028ft)
- **Capacity:** 2 people
- **Use:** for observation only

In 1934, explorers William Beebe and Otis Barton set a record for depth, using their sub *Bathysphere*, when they dived to 928m (3,028ft) underwater.

The *Bathysphere* can be seen today in the New York Aquarium.

Pisces V ocean explorer
(USA 1973–present)

- **Max. depth:** 1,900m (6,280ft)
- **Capacity:** 3 people
- **Submerged speed:** 2kt
- **Use:** for exploration and collection of samples

Danger! Unexploded mines

An MNV, or Mine Neutralization Vehicle, is an ROV designed to disable unexploded mines without putting anyone in danger.

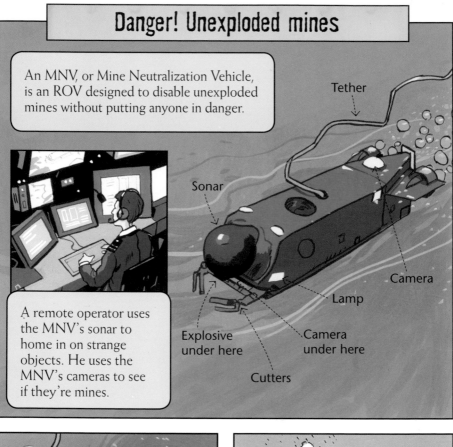

Tether

Sonar

Camera

Lamp

Explosive under here

Camera under here

Cutters

A remote operator uses the MNV's sonar to home in on strange objects. He uses the MNV's cameras to see if they're mines.

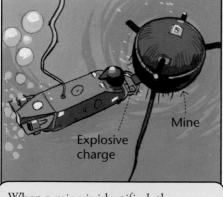

Mine

Explosive charge

When a mine is identified, the MNV can place a small explosive charge on it.

The explosive is detonated by remote control after the MNV has returned safely to its mother ship.

Secrets of the ocean

Oceanographers use unmanned, self-operating subs known as Autonomous Underwater Vehicles (AUVs) to map out large expanses of the seabed.

Sound maps

These AUVs use a technique called side-scan sonar to send out pulses of sound. A computer uses the speed and angle of the echo of each pulse to make a map of the terrain.

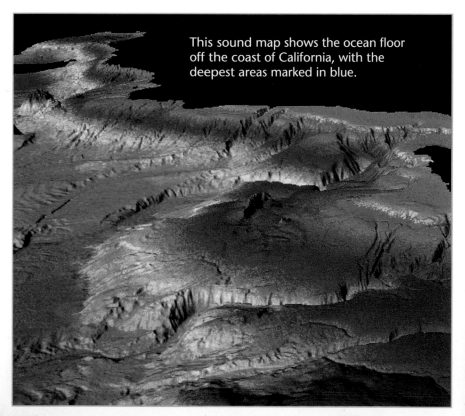

This sound map shows the ocean floor off the coast of California, with the deepest areas marked in blue.

DSV (Deep Submergence Vehicle) *Mir*
(Russia/Finland 1987–present)

- **Max. depth:** 6,000m (3.7 miles)
- **Crew:** 3 people
- **Submerged speed:** 5kt
- **Use:** for deep sea exploration

The *Shinkai 6500* can go deeper than any other submarine currently in service.

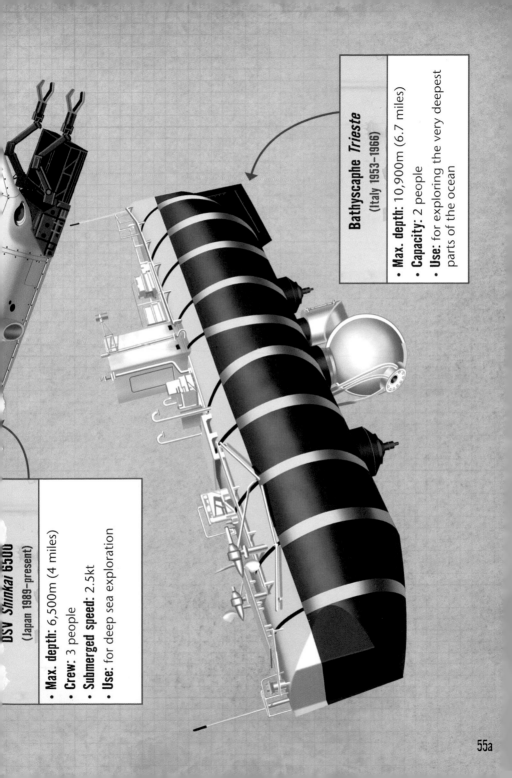

DSV _Shinkai 6500_
(Japan 1989–present)

- **Max. depth:** 6,500m (4 miles)
- **Crew:** 3 people
- **Submerged speed:** 2.5kt
- **Use:** for deep sea exploration

Bathyscaphe _Trieste_
(Italy 1953–1966)

- **Max. depth:** 10,900m (6.7 miles)
- **Capacity:** 2 people
- **Use:** for exploring the very deepest parts of the ocean

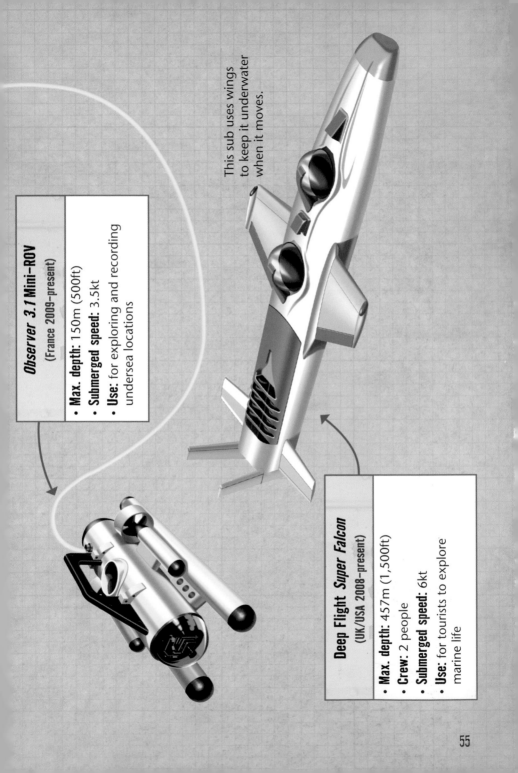

Observer 3.1 Mini-ROV
(France 2009–present)

- **Max. depth:** 150m (500ft)
- **Submerged speed:** 3.5kt
- **Use:** for exploring and recording undersea locations

This sub uses wings to keep it underwater when it moves.

Deep Flight *Super Falcon*
(UK/USA 2008–present)

- **Max. depth:** 457m (1,500ft)
- **Crew:** 2 people
- **Submerged speed:** 6kt
- **Use:** for tourists to explore marine life

55

Mother ship

In the Arctic Ocean, a research team sends down two AUVs, *Puma* and *Jaguar*.

The AUVs dock at these platforms.

Puma uses sonar, lasers and chemical sensors to make a basic terrain map.

Jaguar uses cameras to take detailed pictures of the seabed.

Puma has found an arctic squid.

Finding the *Titanic*

In 1912, the passenger liner *Titanic* hit an iceberg in the Atlantic and sank. For many years, it was thought the ship would never be seen again...

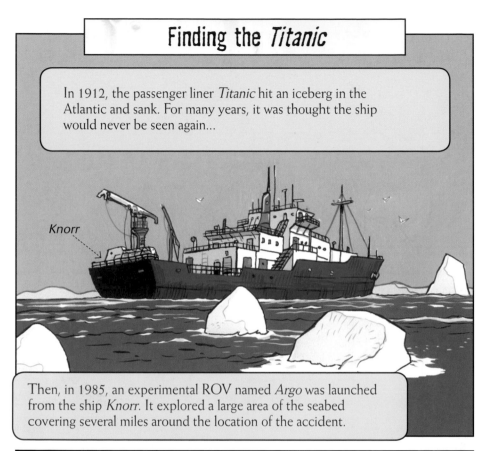

Knorr

Then, in 1985, an experimental ROV named *Argo* was launched from the ship *Knorr*. It explored a large area of the seabed covering several miles around the location of the accident.

After a week, *Argo*'s cameras finally spotted a large hunk of metal. It was soon identified as a ship's boiler – the first sign of the *Titanic*.

The following year, a new team dived in a sub called *Alvin*. The crew saw *Titanic's* hull looming out of the dark.

This time, they spotted furniture and some unopened wine bottles.

Alvin was aided by an ROV called *Jason Junior*, which had a video camera attached.

Jason Junior took this photo, which shows the remains of the Captain's cabin.

Mother ship *Argonaute* carries a NATO rescue vehicle, *Nemo,* to an emergency.

Submarine Rescue Vehicle *Nemo*

Transfer skirt

Emergency rescue

If a sub gets stuck underwater, the captain quickly sends out a distress signal. The crew then has to wait to be rescued by a Submarine Rescue Vehicle (SRV).

In here is a recompression chamber, where rescued submariners can be brought back safely to normal air pressure.

Nemo can be carried by plane and deployed almost anywhere in the world within 72 hours.

How *Nemo* rescues trapped submariners

1. *Nemo* is lowered so its transfer skirt covers the sub's escape hatch. It's held in place by water pressure.

Nemo

Distressed sub

2. Submariners climb through the escape chamber into *Nemo*, which rises to the surface.

Robot rescue vehicles

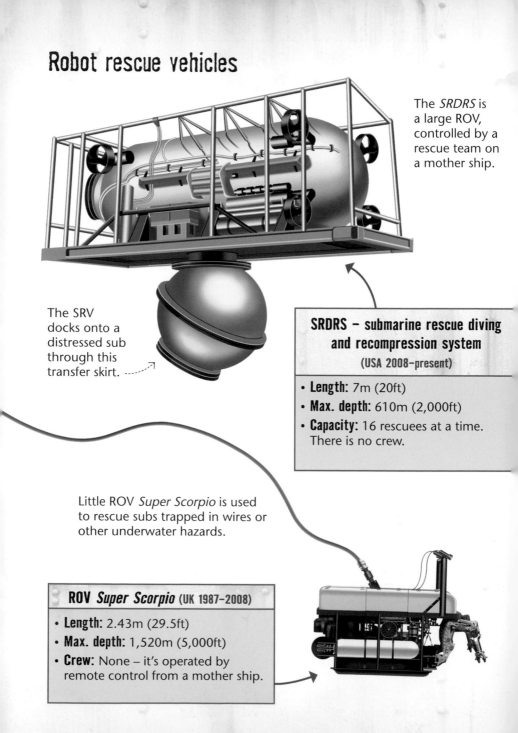

The *SRDRS* is a large ROV, controlled by a rescue team on a mother ship.

The SRV docks onto a distressed sub through this transfer skirt.

SRDRS – submarine rescue diving and recompression system
(USA 2008–present)

- **Length:** 7m (20ft)
- **Max. depth:** 610m (2,000ft)
- **Capacity:** 16 rescuees at a time. There is no crew.

Little ROV *Super Scorpio* is used to rescue subs trapped in wires or other underwater hazards.

ROV *Super Scorpio* (UK 1987–2008)

- **Length:** 2.43m (29.5ft)
- **Max. depth:** 1,520m (5,000ft)
- **Crew:** None – it's operated by remote control from a mother ship.

Rescuing the *Priz*

In August 2005, a Russian mini-submarine named *Priz* got stuck in some nets it was trying to untangle from a hydrophone array. The crewmen were stranded in the freezing North Pacific Ocean.

The *Priz* was connected to a mothership. The crew radioed for a rescue team. Then they had to sit and wait.

36 hours later, a team arrived from Scotland. They used ROV *Super Scorpio* to cut through the tangled nets.

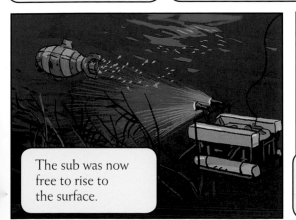

The sub was now free to rise to the surface.

With just hours of air left, the seven-man crew emerged safe and unhurt.

Emergency escape

If there's no time to wait for an SRV, the only option left for the crew of a trapped or disabled submarine is to leave through one of the escape chambers.

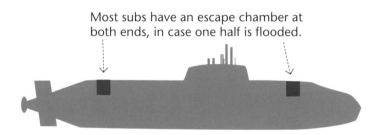

Most subs have an escape chamber at both ends, in case one half is flooded.

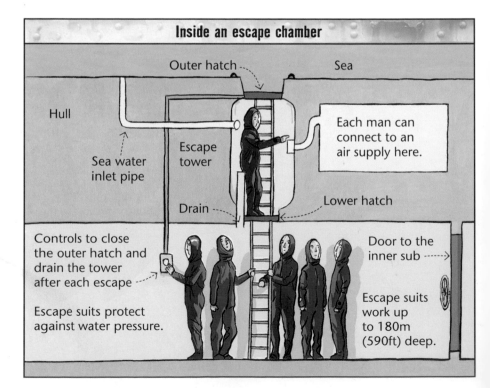

Inside an escape chamber

Outer hatch

Sea

Hull

Sea water inlet pipe

Escape tower

Each man can connect to an air supply here.

Drain

Lower hatch

Controls to close the outer hatch and drain the tower after each escape

Escape suits protect against water pressure.

Door to the inner sub →

Escape suits work up to 180m (590ft) deep.

Getting out

The crew put on their escape suits in the escape chamber. They pull down a ladder to get into the escape tower.

One at a time, each man enters the tower and shuts the lower hatch. Then he fills his suit with air, and floods the tower.

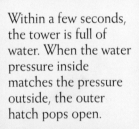

Within a few seconds, the tower is full of water. When the water pressure inside matches the pressure outside, the outer hatch pops open.

Escape suits are very buoyant. This means each man shoots up to the surface in seconds, so they aren't exposed to intense pressure for long.

At the surface, the suit inflates to become a life raft. The air inside keeps the man warm.

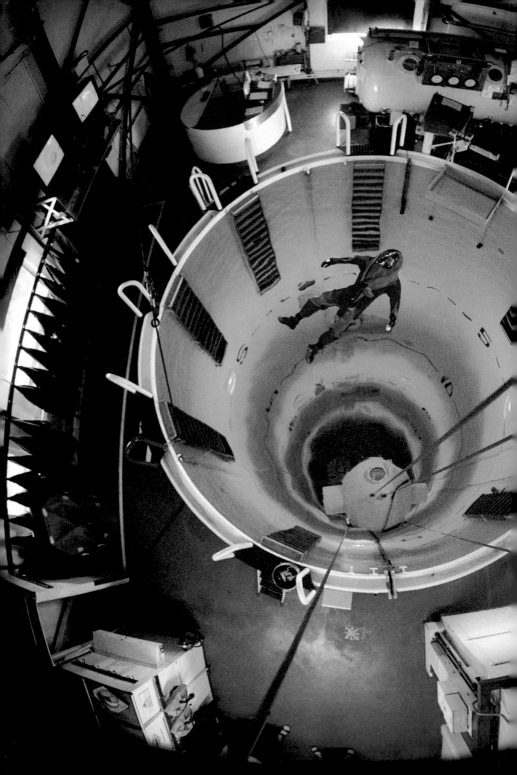

Training submariners

To become a submariner in most countries, you have to join the Navy and serve as a sailor first. Then you have the chance to sign up for an intense submarine training program.

This photo shows an overhead view of the Submarine Escape Training Tank (SETT) in Portsmouth, UK. It's used to help submariners learn how to escape from a disabled sub.

Key to SETT:

❶ Trainee submariner in an escape suit

❷ Simulation of an escape chamber – can be lowered to any depth the tank will allow

❸ Spare escape suit

❹ Recompression chamber, in case of an accident

Training at sea

During patrols, regular exercises are run to make sure the crew members know how to react as quickly and quietly as possible in an emergency.

The *USS Toledo*, a Los Angeles class SSN

In this exercise, the crew must receive a team of Navy SEALs (troops who work on land and at sea) and then take them in secret to a mission point.

MH-60S Seahawk
helicopter

A Navy SEAL slides
down a rope onto
the hull of the sub.

The very first subs

According to legend, the first ever 'submarine' was a glass barrel built by Ancient Greek king Alexander the Great. No one knows if it was actually used.

Alexander the Great being lowered underwater in his barrel

The *Odyssey* (England, 1620)

The first vehicle that worked underwater was a closed-in rowing boat, known as the *Odyssey*. An air tube let the crew breathe up to 5m (15ft) deep.

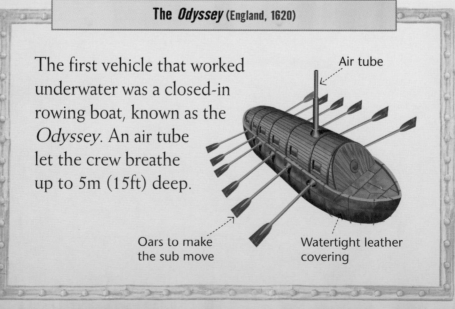

Air tube

Oars to make the sub move

Watertight leather covering

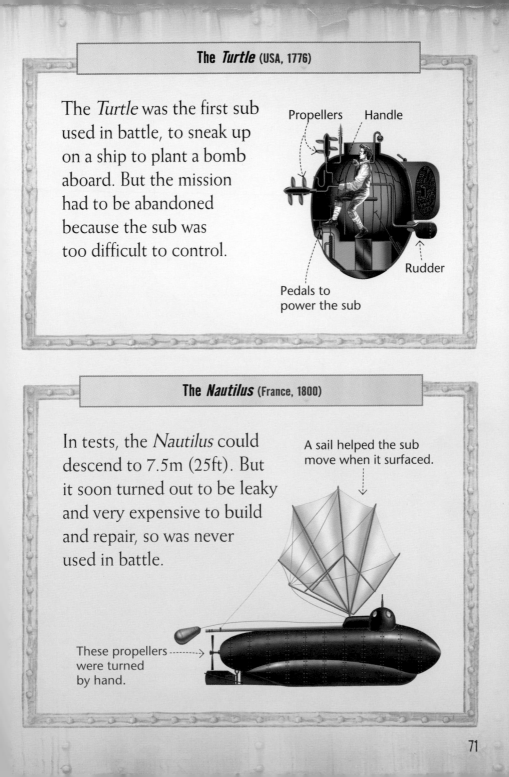

The *Turtle* (USA, 1776)

The *Turtle* was the first sub used in battle, to sneak up on a ship to plant a bomb aboard. But the mission had to be abandoned because the sub was too difficult to control.

Propellers

Handle

Rudder

Pedals to power the sub

The *Nautilus* (France, 1800)

In tests, the *Nautilus* could descend to 7.5m (25ft). But it soon turned out to be leaky and very expensive to build and repair, so was never used in battle.

A sail helped the sub move when it surfaced.

These propellers were turned by hand.

H.L. Hunley (USA, 1864)

The *Hunley* was built and used during the American Civil War. It was the first sub to destroy an enemy ship successfully – but it sank on the way back from its first mission.

Holland 1 (UK, 1901)

American engineer John Holland built a prototype sub in 1897, the first to combine an internal combustion engine to an electric motor. In 1901, the British Royal Navy commissioned him to build *Holland 1*, the first of a small fleet of subs.

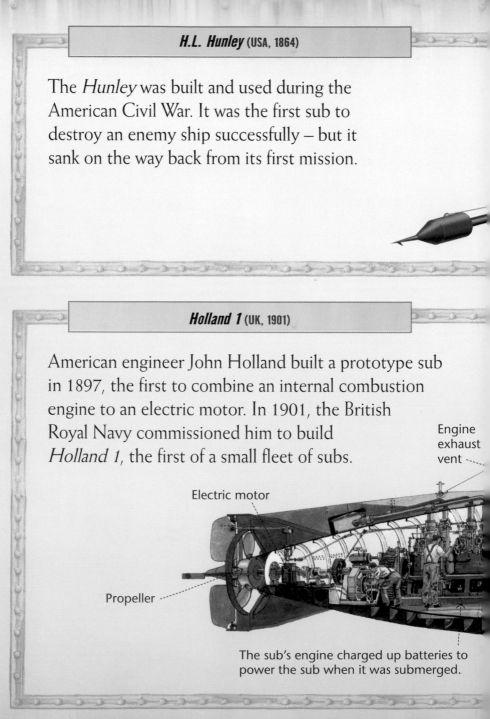

Engine exhaust vent ----

Electric motor

Propeller ----

The sub's engine charged up batteries to power the sub when it was submerged.

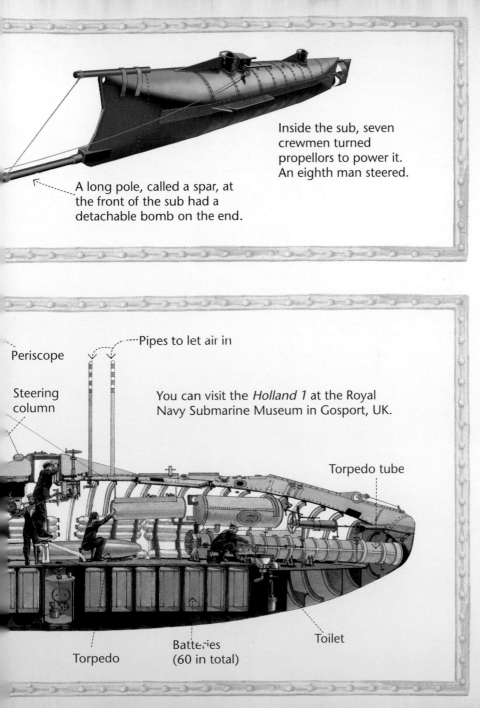

A long pole, called a spar, at the front of the sub had a detachable bomb on the end.

Inside the sub, seven crewmen turned propellors to power it. An eighth man steered.

Periscope

Pipes to let air in

Steering column

You can visit the *Holland 1* at the Royal Navy Submarine Museum in Gosport, UK.

Torpedo tube

Torpedo

Batteries (60 in total)

Toilet

Submarines on the internet

There are lots of websites with information about submarines old and new. At the Usborne Quicklinks website, you'll find links to some great sites where you can:

- Find out where you can step inside an actual submarine

- Read about the exploits of heroic submariners from the First and Second World Wars

- See a list of every submarine used in the Second World War

- Take a virtual tour of the oceans as if you were inside a submarine

When using the internet please follow the internet safety guidelines displayed on the Usborne Quicklinks Website. The recommended websites in Usborne Quicklinks are regularly reviewed and updated, but Usborne Publishing Ltd. is not responsible for the content or availability of any website other than its own. We recommend that children are supervised while using the internet.

The sub *U-995*, a surviving Type VIIC sub from the Second World War, can be visited in Laboe, Schleswig-Holstein, Germany.

For links to websites all about submarines, go to the Usborne Quicklinks Website at **www.usborne-quicklinks.com** and enter the keyword **submarines**.

Glossary

This glossary explains some of the words used in this book. If a word is written in *italic* type, it has an entry of its own.

AUV Autonomous Underwater Vehicle, an unmanned *submarine* that can pilot itself.

ballast tank A tank that can be filled with air or water, to let a *sub* float or sink.

bow The front of a ship or *sub*.

buoy A marker that floats on the surface of the sea.

class *Submarines* of the same type are described as being part of a class.

depth charge An explosive set to go off when it reaches a certain depth in the sea.

diesel A type of fuel.

electrolysis A chemical process that uses electricity to break water apart, releasing oxygen gas.

escape suit A full-body suit that holds air for the wearer to breathe and to keep warm.

hatch A doorway into or out of a *submarine*.

HMS Her (or His) Majesty's Ship, a prefix given to ships and *subs* in the British Royal Navy.

hull The outer wall of a ship or *sub*.

hydrophone An underwater microphone, used to pick up sounds in the sea.

hydroplane Part of a *submarine* that controls depth.

knots Nautical miles per hour, a measure of speed in water.

masts Equipment that can be raised or lowered from the sail, such as a *periscope* or radio transmitter.

midget sub A small, sneaky *submarine*.

mine An explosive device, set to detonate when hit.

missile A flying weapon, often guided automatically to hit a target.

mother ship A ship that carries a *sub* out to sea, and provides technical support.

nuclear engine An engine that gets power from the energy given off by *radioactive* materials.

nuclear missile A hugely powerful explosive that uses *radioactive* materials.

periscope A *mast* containing lenses and mirrors that enables a viewer to see outside a *sub*, and above the waves.

PD Periscope Depth, the maximum depth at which a *sub* can raise its *periscope* above the surface of the water.

radioactive A substance that breaks down and gives off energy.

recompression A method of safely bringing people to normal air pressure who have been subjected to great *water pressure* in the sea.

ROV Remotely Operated Vehicle, an unmanned sub piloted by an operator on board a *mother ship* or *sub*.

scrubbers Chemicals that absorb carbon dioxide, used to keep the air breathable inside a *submerged sub*.

SEAL US Navy troops who are trained for action on Sea, Air and Land.

SETT Submarine Escape Training Tank, a deep tank of water that *submariners* use to practice escaping from a *submerged sub*.

side-scan sonar A way of using *sonar* to make maps of the seabed.

sonar A method of detecting sounds, and the name for the equipment used for this.

SRV Submarine Rescue Vehicle.

SSBN A nuclear-powered *sub* that carries long range ballistic *nuclear missiles*.

SSGN A nuclear-powered *sub* that carries short range guided missiles.

SSK A conventional (non-nuclear) attack *sub* that carries *torpedoes*.

SSN A nuclear-powered attack *submarine* that carries *torpedoes*.

stern the back of a ship or *sub*.

submarine, or sub A ship that can travel underwater as well as on the surface.

submariner A person who lives or works on a *submarine*. The word is commonly pronounced 'sub-MAriner' in the UK, and 'subma-Reener' in the US.

submerged Beneath the surface of the sea.

submersible A *sub* that relies on a *mother ship* for support.

swim-out chamber A chamber that can be flooded with air or water to let people in and out of a *submerged sub*.

torpedo An underwater *missile*.

turbine Part of an engine that converts energy into electricity.

USS United States Ship, a prefix given to ships and *subs* in the US Navy.

USSR Union of Soviet Socialist Republics, a Eurasian nation, principally including Russia, that existed between 1922 and 1991.

U-boat Short for *Unterseeboot*, the German word for *submarine*.

water pressure The force of water pushing against a *sub*. The deeper the sub, the greater the pressure.

Index

Page numbers marked with an 'a' are found underneath the flap on that page.

Acknowledgements

Every effort has been made to trace and acknowledge ownership of copyright. If any rights have been omitted, the publishers offer to rectify this in any future editions following notification. The publishers are grateful to the following individuals and organizations for their permission to reproduce material on the following pages: (t=top, b=bottom)

cover Los Angeles class SSN © Corbis RF/Alamy; **p1** © Matthias Kulka/Corbis; **p2-3** © Corbis; **p8-9 and p8a-9a** © BAE systems 2008; **p10** © www.universalnewsandsport.com; **p14** © BAE systems 2008; **p15** U.S. Navy photo by Chief Photographer's Mate Andrew McKaskle; **p17** © Scott MacQuarrie/Alamy; **p19 (t)** © Corbis, **(b)** © AKG; **p20** U.S. Navy photo by Mass Communication Specialist 1st Class Fernando Allen; **p21** U.S. Navy photo by Journalist 1st Class James Pinsky; **p23** © Corbis; **p28** © Getty images; **p32-33** © Hulton-Deutsch Collection/Corbis; **p34-35** Imperial War Museum A7745; **p36-37** Tony Bryan, *Imperial Japanese Navy Submarines 1941-45* © Osprey Publishing; **p42-43** US Navy graphic; **p44-45** U. S. Navy photo by Chief Yeoman Alphonso Braggs; **p48** Photo courtesy of Defenseimagery.mil and Lt. Bob Struth, U.S. Navy. Use does not imply or constitute U.S. Department of Defense endorsement; **p49** U.S. Navy photo; **p50-51** © Mark Deeble & Victoria Stone/Photolibrary.com; **p52** Alexis Rosenfeld/Science Photo Library; **p56** W. Haxby, Lamont-Doherty Earth Observatory/Science Photo Library; **p57** © Woods Hole Oceanographic Institution; **p58** courtesy of Lori Johnston, RMS Titanic Expedition 2003, NOAA-OE; **p60-61** © Jonathan Powis; **p66-67** Photograph by: Gary Davies, Royal Navy; Crown Copyright/MOD, image from www.photos.mod.uk. Reproduced with the permission of the Controller of Her Majesty's Stationery Office; **p68-69** © U.S. Navy photo by Journalist 3rd Class Davis J. Anderson; **p72-73** courtesy of the Royal Navy Submarine Museum, Gosport; **p74-75** © Arco Images GmbH/Alamy

Additional illustrations by Zoe Wray
Additional editorial material by Gill Doherty and Louie Stowell
Additional designs by Jessica Johnson
Digital design by John Russell and Nick Wakeford
Picture research by Ruth King